Editor

Mary S. Jones

Managing Editor

Ina Massler Levin, M.A.

Illustrator

Blanca Apodaca

Cover Artist

Brenda DiAntonis

Art Manager

Kevin Barnes

Art Director

CJae Froshay

Imaging

Rosa C. See

Publisher

Mary D. Smith, M.S. Ed.

Author

Shelle Russell

Teacher Created Resources, Inc.

6421 Industry Way

Westminster, CA 92683

www.teachercreated.com

ISBN-1-4206-3981-1

©2005 Teacher Created Resources, Inc.

Reprinted, 2006

Made in U.S.A.

Table of Contents

Introduction

Mind Twisters is a creative, motivational book used to stimulate children's minds! Each page was developed to reinforce the essential strategies and skills that are being taught in classrooms today. The pages may be reproduced for individual or group use. You may choose to make them into overheads, use them at learning centers, or use them to reinforce skills that need additional practice. This art-filled book is divided into 11 sections titled *Numbers, Sequence, Patterns, Riddles, Words, Mazes, Logical and Critical Thinking Skills, Test Your Memory, Hidden Pictures, Strange but Amazing Stories,* and *Take Your Pick.* Having separate sections allows you to pick and choose activities and/or enrichments best suited to the needs of your students.

✏ Numbers

The mind twisters in this section involve mathematical skills such as counting, addition, subtraction, and higher-order thinking skills.

✏ Sequence

This section gives excellent practice in the following skills: time, order of events, alphabetical order, and comparing numbers.

✏ Patterns

The activities here involve both number and picture patterns. Read on to find out "what comes next!"

✏ Riddles

With the activities in this section, students are detectives and learn to "crack the code" in order to answer the funny riddles.

✏ Words

The mind twisters in this section require students to unscramble words, break down words, and try to make new words. These are great for spelling practice!

✏ Mazes

Can you reach the end? Students have to think hard to complete the mazes in this section.

✏ Logical and Critical Thinking Skills

All of the activities in this section give students pictures and clues to help them figure out the puzzles. Be careful! Don't let their minds get too twisted!

✏ Test Your Memory

In this section, students will be looking at pictures and using their memories to help them answer the questions.

✏ Hidden Pictures

Don't let the pictures fool you. Hidden in these mind twisters are some "out of sight" objects.

✏ Strange but Amazing Stories

The activities in this section allow students to become the authors of their very own funny stories.

✏ Take Your Pick

With the activities in this section, students will be given word choices to complete the tasks.

Mind Twisters are fun; let them twist your child's mind today!

Who's Driving 20?

Add each group of numbers on the cars below. The funniest clown is driving the car whose sum equals 20. Which car is that clown driving? Color that car.

$2 + 3 + 7 + 5 = \boxed{}$

Car 1

$3 + 4 + 2 + 9 = \boxed{}$

Car 2

$9 + 3 + 2 + 6 = \boxed{}$

Car 3

$7 + 3 + 3 + 4 = \boxed{}$

Car 4

$2 + 7 + 9 + 7 = \boxed{}$

Car 5

$1 + 3 + 4 + 5 = \boxed{}$

Car 6

4

Crazy Canisters

All of Charlie's canisters fell off the counter. Can you help put them in number order from the greatest to the least? Write the answers on the lines below.

1. _____

2. _____

3. _____

4. _____

5. _____

6. _____

7. _____

Shapes All Over

Shapes are hidden everywhere below. Can you find the correct number of each shape?

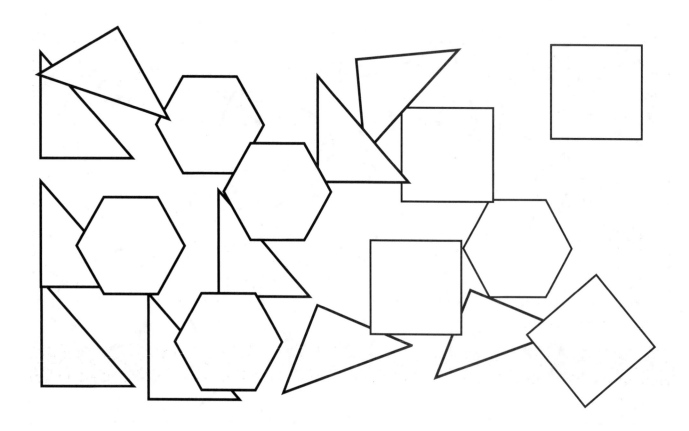

How many triangles? _____

How many hexagons? _____

How many squares? _____

Farm Squabble

Uncle Ted's animals got loose all over the barnyard, and he forgot how many animals he has. Can you fill in the graph below to help him count his animals?

Graph the animals below.

	1	2	3	4	5	6
pigs						
cows						
sheep						
chickens						
dogs						

What animal does he have the most of? _____

How many more sheep does he have than dogs? _____

How many animals does Uncle Ted have in all? _____

Pirate Pete's Buried Treasure

Pirate Pete has discovered a map for buried treasure. It says, "Always follow the path whose number is greater than the one you are on." Can you help him find his way?

Stompin' Boots

Juan and his buddies plan to buy these boots for hiking. Before they can take them home, they have to solve the math problems on each boot. Write the number in each box that will make each number sentence correct. The first one has been done for you.

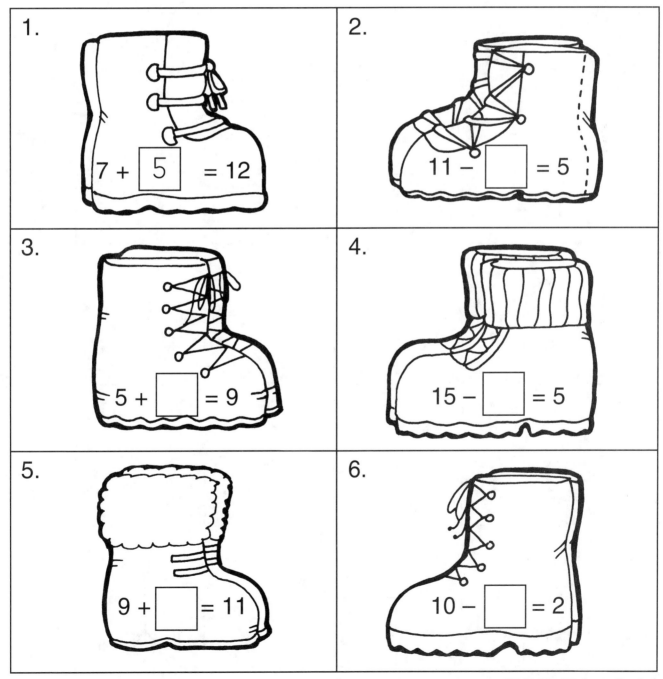

1. $7 + \boxed{5} = 12$

2. $11 - \boxed{} = 5$

3. $5 + \boxed{} = 9$

4. $15 - \boxed{} = 5$

5. $9 + \boxed{} = 11$

6. $10 - \boxed{} = 2$

Math Wizard

Tiny Jessica loves math facts. Fill in the blank boxes as you follow the path. If the operation says add, add the two numbers together. If it says subtract, take away the second number and fill in the answer box. The first answer box has been done for you. Help her get to the end of the path as fast as you can. Can you beat her time of one minute?

Start ⟹ | 5 | – | 2 | = | 3 | + | 1 | =

4 | + | | = | 3 | – | | = | 2 | +

=

| – | 1 | = | | – | 2 | = | | +

1

| = | 1 | + | | = | 4 | + | | =

–

2 | = | | – | 3 | = | | Finish!

Can You Dew It?

Look at the picture below. Count each of the items listed and put the number next to the word. Use these numbers to add or subtract the math problems that follow.

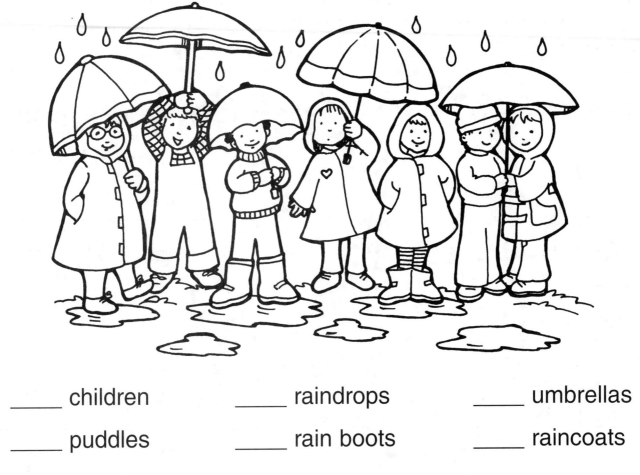

____ children   ____ raindrops   ____ umbrellas

____ puddles   ____ rain boots   ____ raincoats

Add or subtract the following using the numbers above to help you.

Add	Subtract	Add	Subtract
___ children	___ raindrops	___ umbrellas	___ puddles
+ ___ rain boots	− ___ puddles	+ ___ raincoats	− ___ rain boots
_____	_____	_____	_____

Bubba's Books

Bubba's books fell off his bookshelf. He likes them to be in alphabetical order. Can you put them back in alphabetical order for him? Write the titles of the books on the lines below.

1. _____

2. _____

3. _____

4. _____

5. _____

Beach Days

Can you number these pictures to show what happened first, second, and so on? Write the numbers (1–6) in the squares to show the order in which the events happened.

Who's First to the Movies?

Sally, Sam, Sarah, and Sandy went to the movies. Who is first in line? Who is second, third, and last? Use the clues below to help you.

Clues

The first person in line is a boy.
Sarah is holding a bag of popcorn.
Sandy is between Sam and Sally.
Sally is wearing shorts.

Who's first? _____   Who's third? _____

Who's second? _____   Who's last? _____

Watch Out for the Watches!

Brandon collects watches. All of them show a different time. Put the times in order starting with 12:00.

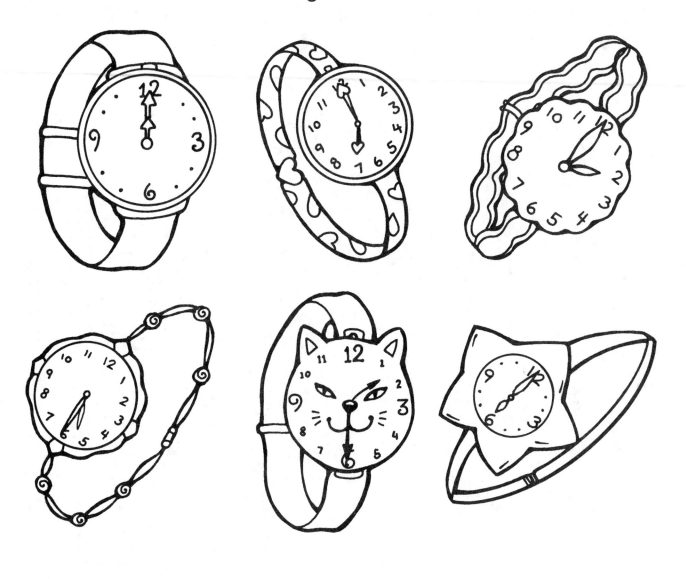

1. _____12:00_____   4. _____

2. _____   5. _____

3. _____   6. _____

Confusing Candies

Missy sells different kinds of candy. Her shelves are set up in order from the cheapest candy to the most expensive candy. Can you help her put the candies in the right order? Write the money amounts in order from cheapest to most expensive on the lines below.

Cheapest

_____

_____

_____

_____

_____

Most Expensive

16

Numbers Gone Wild!

The runners from the race got mixed up. Can you put their numbers back in order so the race can start? Order them from the smallest number to the greatest. Write your answers on the lines below.

1. _____   5. _____

2. _____   6. _____

3. _____   7. _____

4. _____

Month Mania

Mrs. Stillman bumped her calendar. All of her months fell down. Can you help her put them back into the right order? Write them in the correct order on the lines below.

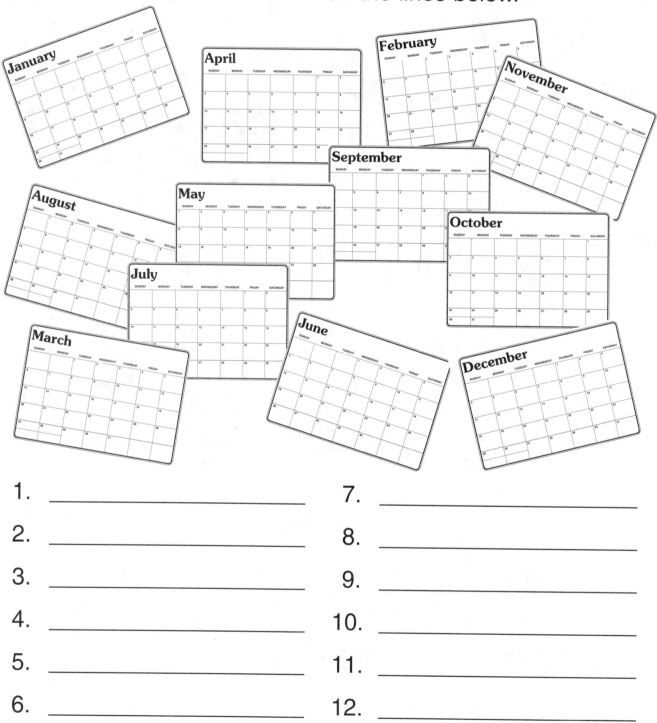

1. _____

2. _____

3. _____

4. _____

5. _____

6. _____

7. _____

8. _____

9. _____

10. _____

11. _____

12. _____

Pizza Puzzler

Sandra has a puzzle of pepperoni pizza. The pepperoni slices are making her confused. Can you help her finish the puzzle? Circle the piece that will fit into the missing spot.

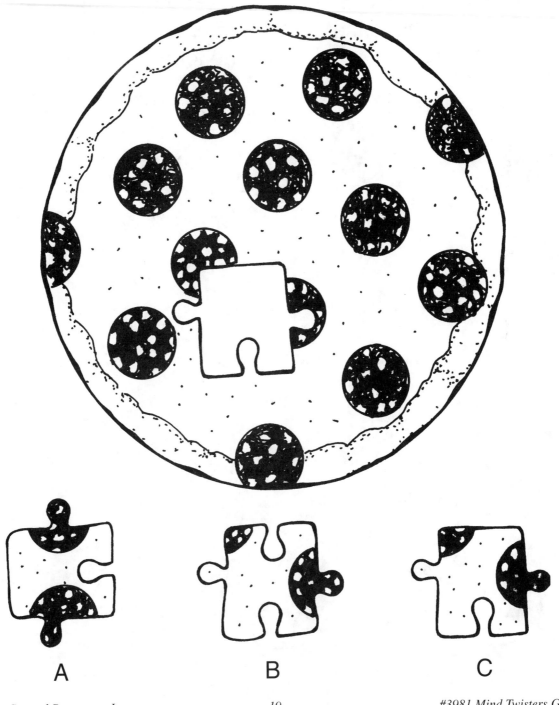

A   B   C

#3981 Mind Twisters Grade 1

Matching Cans

Sal made many cans in art class. He made two of each pattern. For example, he made one can with a white heart and one with a black heart. Can you find the seven pairs of cans with the matching patterns? Draw a line from one can to its matching can until you have found all of the matches. There are a few cans that do not match with anything, so be careful! The first one has been done for you.

What Comes Next?

Maya loves to draw patterns. Can you finish the patterns that she has started? Write or draw what comes next in the box.

1. 123 123123 123 123123 123 123123 123

2.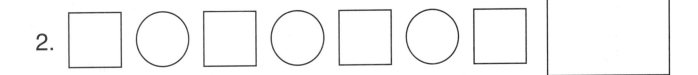

3.

4.

5.

Maybelle's Quilt

Maybelle is making a design for her quilt. Use the pattern she started below to help her complete her design.

Billy's Hideout

Billy is using different things to make patterns at his hideout. Can you complete Billy's five patterns before he returns? Finish the pictures to complete each pattern. Each pattern starts at the top of the page, and ends at the bottom.

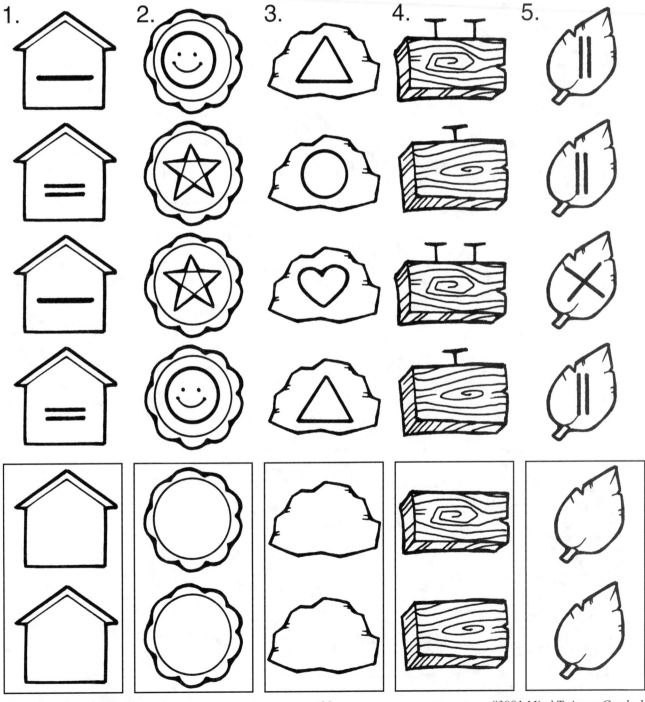

Cookies Like This!

Lulu wants to make tray arrangements with her cookies. Can you help her complete the patterns for each tray? Finish the cookies to complete the pattern on each tray.

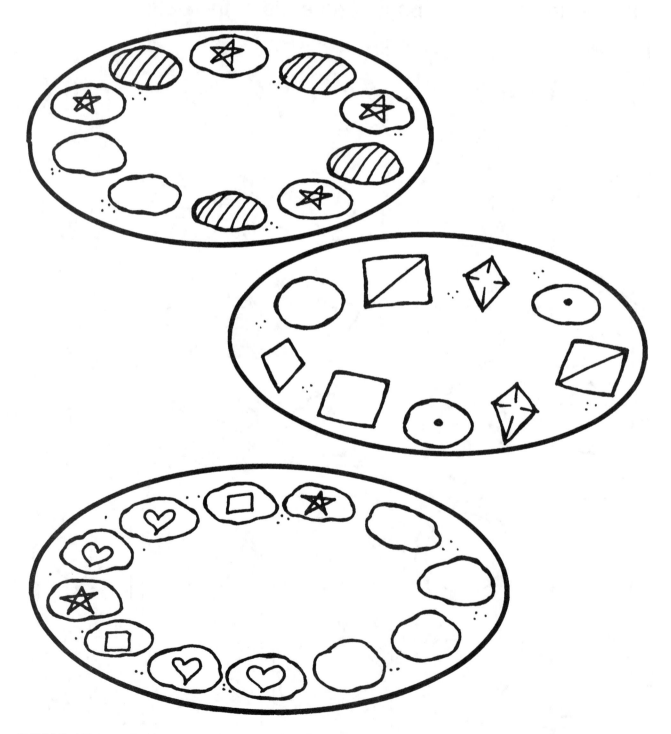

24

Skip It!

Can you help complete the patterns below? Fill in each blank with the missing number.

1. 5 ____ 15 ____ 25 ____ ____ 40 ____ 50

2. 10 20 30 40 ____ ____ 70 ____ ____ 100

3. 24 ____ 28 30 ____ ____ 36 ____ ____ ____ 44 46 ____ 50

4. 25 ____ 35 ____ ____ 50 ____ ____ ____ 70

It's Your Ball

Look at the patterns below. Can you pick the ball that will come next? Choose the correct letter and write it in the empty shape.

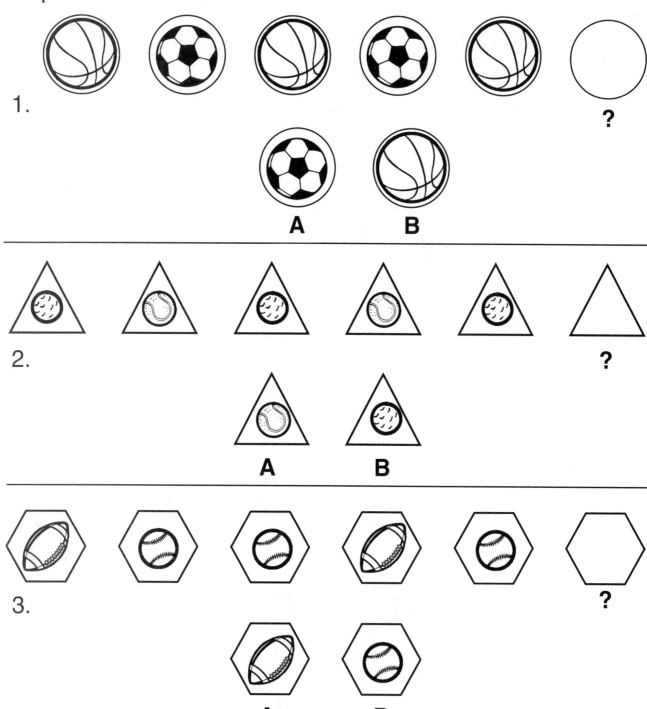

26

Cloud Bursters

Look at the clouds in each row. Can you guess which cloud will come next? Circle the cloud on the right that will continue the pattern.

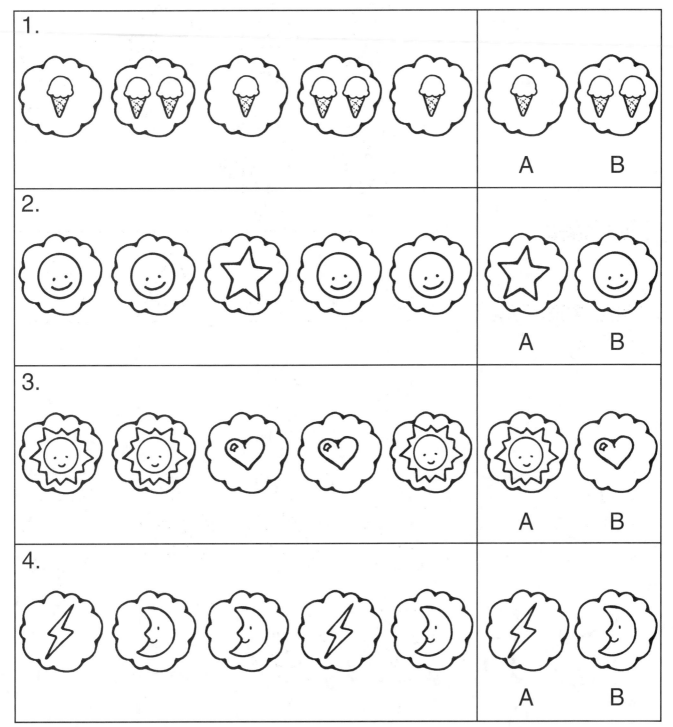

Cracking Up Over Patterns

Look at the patterns below. Complete the patterns by drawing what would come next in the box.

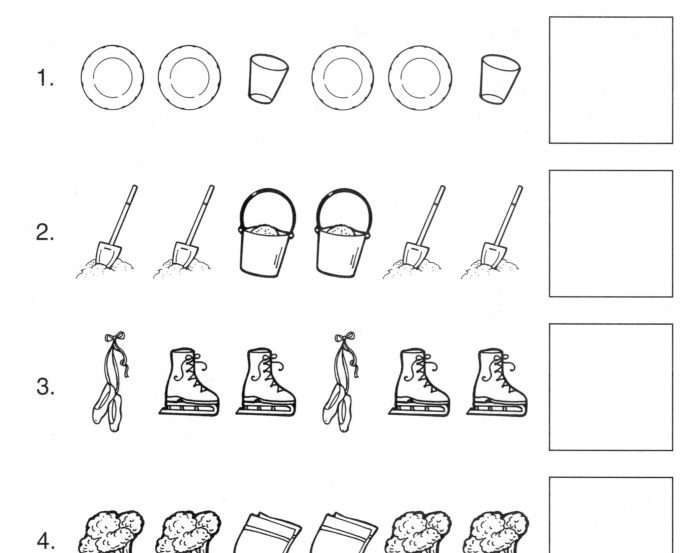

1.

2.

3.

4.

5.

Mama Tree

Use the code below to help you solve the riddle. Write each letter below the circle to solve it.

What did the mama pine tree say to the baby pine trees?

S T O P

N E E D L I N G

E A C H

O T H E R !

Answer Code

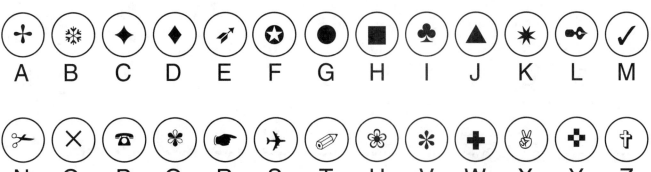

| A | B | C | D | E | F | G | H | I | J | K | L | M |

| N | O | P | Q | R | S | T | U | V | W | X | Y | Z |

Snowman's Good Grades

Use the code below to help you solve the riddle. Write each letter below the shape to solve it.

Why did the snowman get straight A's?

___ ___   ___ ___ ___   ___

___ ___ ___ ___ – ___ ___ ___ – ___ ___ ___ !

Answer Code

A B C D E F G H I J K L M

N O P Q R S T U V W X Y Z

Hummingbirds

Use the code below to help you solve the riddle. Write each letter below the shape to solve it.

Why do hummingbirds hum?

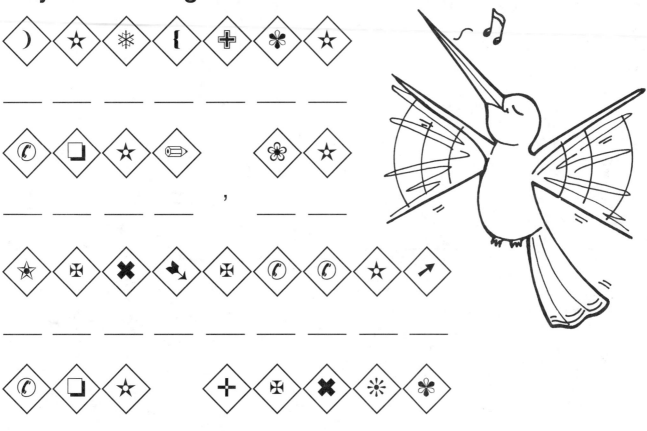

Answer Code

{	)	❄	✸	☆	★	↙	□	❸	✳	🐀	❷	▶
A	B	C	D	E	F	G	H	I	J	K	L	M

↗	✠	✔	☎	✖	✻	ⓒ	✚	❀	✛	❾	✏	①
N	O	P	Q	R	S	T	U	V	W	X	Y	Z

Frog Drink

Use the code below to help you solve the riddle. Write each letter below the square to solve it.

What do frogs drink?

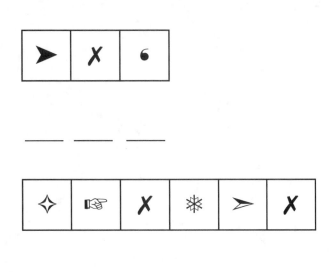

___ ___ ___

___ ___ ___ ___ ___ ___

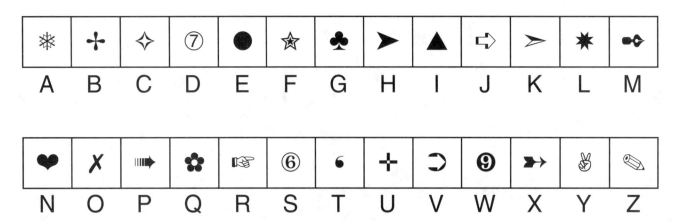

Answer Code

❋	✛	✦	⑦	●	☆	♣	➤	▲	⇨	➢	✳	⊷
A	B	C	D	E	F	G	H	I	J	K	L	M

❤	✗	⇛	❀	☞	⑥	'	✛	⊃	❾	➥	✌	✐
N	O	P	Q	R	S	T	U	V	W	X	Y	Z

Frog Wear

Use the code below to help you solve the riddle. Write each letter below the shape to solve it.

What kind of shoes do frogs like?

___ ___ ___ ___ - ___ ___ ___ ___

___ ___ ___ ___ ___ ___ ___

Answer Code

↠	♠	♦	✳	◻	☆	✱	♣	⬿	▼	◆	◈	↕
A	B	C	D	E	F	G	H	I	J	K	L	M

✺	↗	✔	☎	♥	ℰ	⬿	⅁	✈	☞	→	✚	⊛
N	O	P	Q	R	S	T	U	V	W	X	Y	Z

Fishing for Toast

Use the code below to help you solve the riddle. Write each letter below the shape to solve the it.

What kind of fish goes well with toast?

_____ _____ _____ _____ _____ _____

_____ _____ _____ _____ .

Answer Code

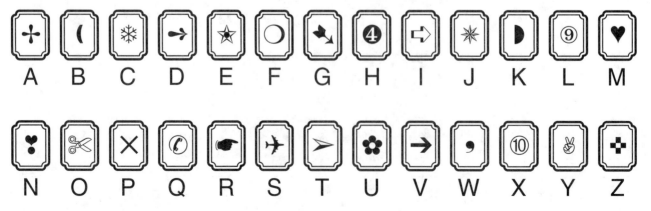

Snowflake Students

Use the code below to help you solve the riddle. Write each letter below the shape to solve it.

Why do snowflakes make bad students?

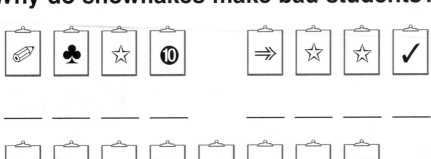

Answer Code

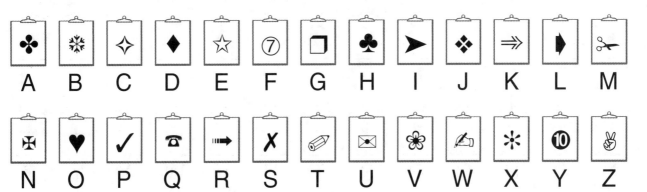

Sparrow in the Library

Use the code below to help you solve the riddle. Write each letter below the books to solve it.

Why did the sparrow fly into the library?

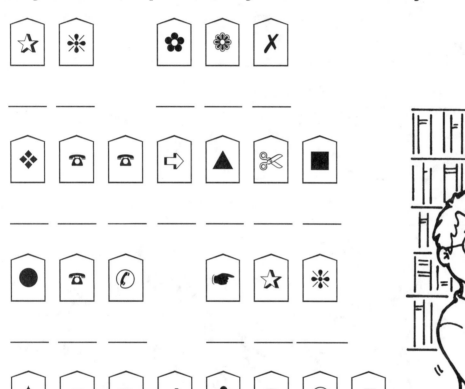

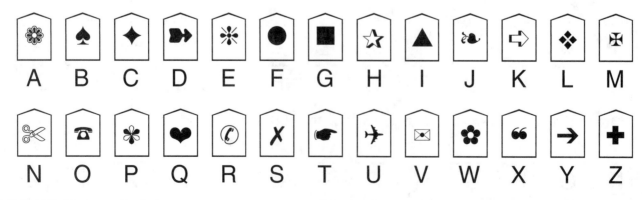

Answer Code

A	B	C	D	E	F	G	H	I	J	K	L	M

N	O	P	Q	R	S	T	U	V	W	X	Y	Z

Words in Words!

A carpenter is a person who builds things with wood. How many words can you find hidden inside the word *carpenter*? Write one word on each wooden board below. Look for words that have three or more letters only! An example has been done for you.

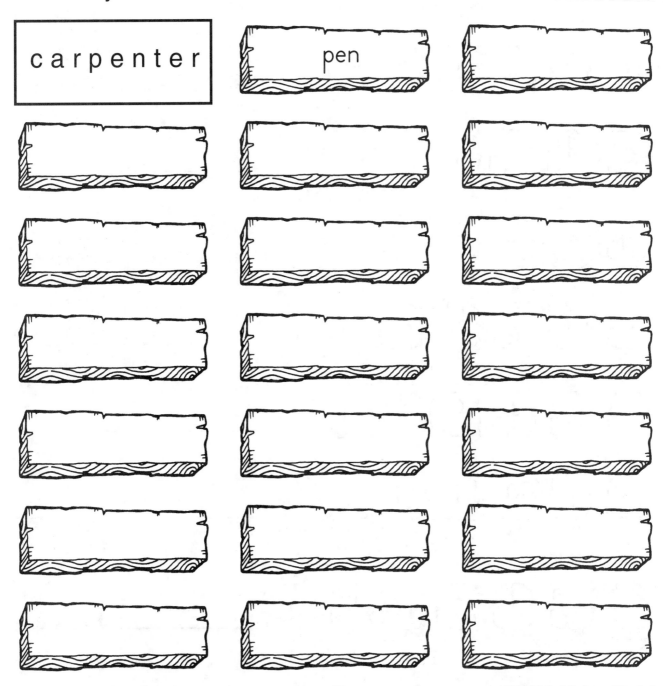

c a r p e n t e r

pen

Scrambled Up Zoo

Amanda visited the zoo on Saturday. She made a list of the animals she saw. When she went home, her little brother tore up the list. Help her unscramble the letters so she can remember the names of the animals she saw. Hint: The circled letter is the first letter of each animal name.

(m) k o y n e _____

o (l) n i _____

g (t) e r i _____

p i p (h) o _____

i e f (g) f a r _____

r o (g) l a i l _____

h o l i n p (d) _____

What's the Same?

The words in each column below have something in common. Can you find out what it is?

Column 1	Column 2	Column 3	Column 4	Column 5
with	would	rats	little	she
them	you	star	his	he
path	out	arts	like	we
they	your	tars	said	see

What's the same in …

Column 1? _____

Column 2? _____

Column 3? _____

Column 4? _____

Column 5? _____

Baking Poem

See if you can unscramble the mixed-up words in this short poem. Use the box next to each silly word to write the word it really is. Next, read the poem out loud as quickly as you can!

Making chocolate **dum** _____ pies is our favorite

gnith _____ ;

As we dance around in mud – this is what we **gnis** _____ .

One, two, **pih** _____ , hooray.

Three, four, make my **yad** _____ .

Five, six, chocolate **esaelp** _____ .

Pour the **spihc** _____ in now with ease.

Pour some water, **xim** _____ the mud.

Pack it in a **nit** _____ .

Smack and **kcap** _____ , stack the **dum** _____ ,

Smash it **nwod** _____ again.

Mud **seip** _____ , mud pies, are so great to make.

Next week, next **keew** _____ , we'll make another

ekac _____ !

Animal Language

These animals forgot what they were doing. Read each question and circle the letter that will best help the animal know the right sound to make.

1. If you were a cow, you might be:

   A. stewing

   B. mewing

   C. mooing

2. If you were a chicken, you would probably be:

   A. pecking

   B. necking

   C. checking

3. If you were a duck, you would surely:

   A. smack

   B. quack

   C. stack

4. If you were a horse, you would be sure to:

   A. neigh

   B. play

   C. stay

5. If you were a dog, you would certainly:

   A. mark

   B. bark

   C. park

In the Barn

The words on this page are stuck in the boards of the barn. Can you help the farmer by unscrambling his farm words? Write the ten words on the haystacks below the barn.

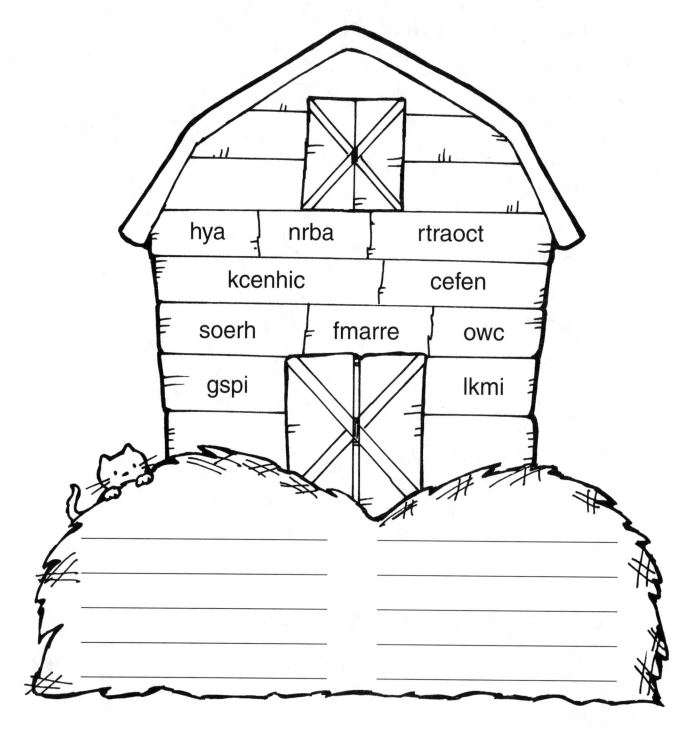

hya   nrba   rtraoct

kcenhic   cefen

soerh   fmarre   owc

gspi   lkmi

Tell the Truth

Read each sentence below. Only one of the sentences is true. Which one is it? Circle the one that is true. Next, cross out the word or number that makes each sentence untrue and add the word or number that will make it correct.

1. Cats have three legs.

2. George Washington was the first United States President.

3. The U.S. flag is red, white, and black.

4. A five-dollar bill is shaped like a circle.

5. Pine trees are blue.

6. The opposite of *up* is *run*.

7. Chocolate ice cream is usually green.

8. The alphabet has 28 letters.

9. *A, E, I, O,* and *U* are consonants.

10. Bicycles generally have twelve wheels.

Alphabet Soup

Search for words in the bowl of soup below. Circle or color each word as you find it. Can you find them all? One word is not in the bowl of soup. Which word is missing? _____

MADE	THEIR	KNOW	WITH	YOU
YOUR	FROM	DOWN	THAT	THEY

Earthworms

Search for words inside the word *earthworms*. Write each word that you discover on a worm below. Each word must have three or more letters. Remember, only use each word one time! An example has been done for you.

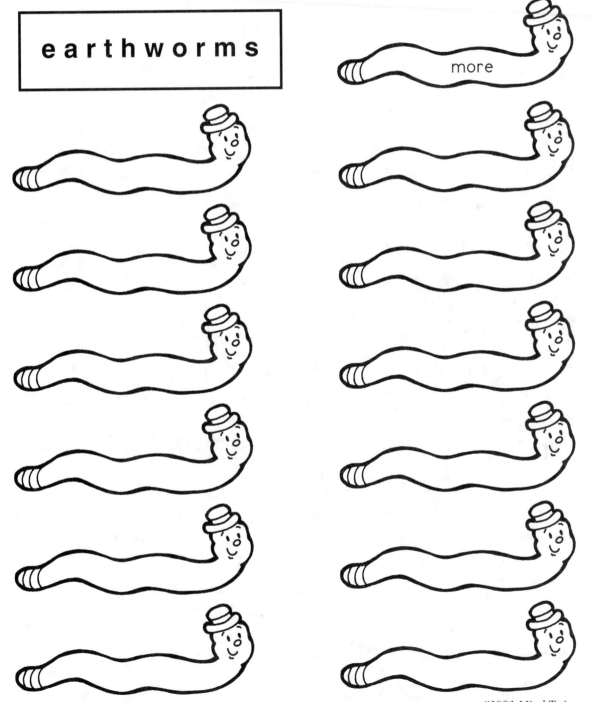

earthworms

more

Tangled Ropes

Four children brought ropes to the playground. They got tangled up. Use a pencil to follow the ropes from the hands of the children to see which rope belongs to which child. Write each child's number in the box next to his or her rope.

46

I Scream! You Scream! We All Scream for Ice Cream!

It is a hot day. Use your pencil to get from one end of the maze to the other to find your way to the ice cream cone! If you run into a dead-end, then you must try a different way.

House on Fire!

Will the fire engine get to the fire in time? Use your pencil to trace a path from the fire engine to the burning house to find the fastest way to the fire! If you run into a dead-end, then you must try a different way. Hurry!

To the Top of the Mast!

Race the pirates to the top of the mast. Use your pencil to get from one end of the maze to the other to find your way to the top! If you run into a dead-end, then you must try a different way.

RRR!!! Race'em!

Which car belongs on which track? Use your pencil to get from the car to the end of each track! Can you untangle the tracks to find out who is the winner? Write the car number on the ribbon at the end of each path.

1st Place

2nd Place

3rd Place

Star Search

Which path leads to star in the middle? Use your pencil to trace each line on the maze. If you do not get to the center square, then try again until you find the line that reaches the middle.

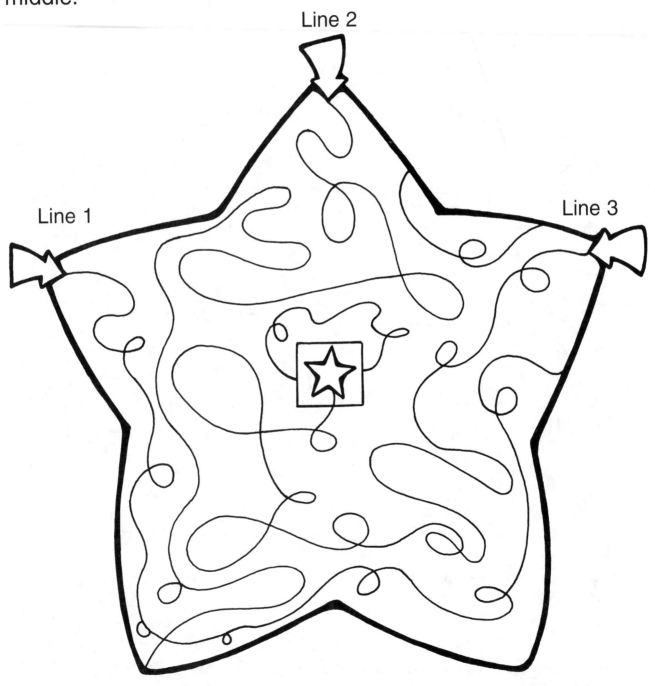

Beaver Dam

Mr. Beaver wants to get through his twigs quickly. Use your pencil to get from the top of the beaver dam to the inside. If you run into a dead-end, then you must try a different way to get there! Can you help him get home in time for dinner?

Who's Up First?

Fernando, Frankie, Freddy, and Filbert are on the same baseball team. The coach put them in order to bat, but he forgot the order. Can you help out? Use the clues to solve the problem. Write the answers on the lines below.

Clues

The weakest hitter, who bats last, is wearing his hat backwards.

The second batter, who is great at bunting, is wearing his hat sideways.

The first batter is a fast runner and a great hitter. He is holding two bats.

Freddy bats before Fernando.

| **Fernando** | **Frankie** | **Freddy** | **Filbert** |

Batting order:

1. _____   3. _____

2. _____   4. _____

What's Your Flavor?

Super Scooper Ice Cream Shop is having a sale on four different types of ice cream. You want to order cones for yourself and your three friends: Jennifer, Amber, and Ashley. Each of you must pick a different flavor. Can you help figure out which friend will get which flavor? Read the clues below to help you. Write the answers on the lines below.

Clues

You get the flavor that is left.

Jennifer likes small chunks of chocolate.

Ashley adores the flavor that reminds her of sandwiches.

Amber likes the flavor with a caramel river in the middle.

 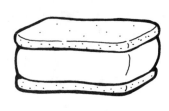  

Chocolate Chunk **Ice Cream Sandwich** **Vanilla Caramel** **Strawberry Crunch**

1. You get _____.

2. Jennifer likes _____.

3. Ashley chooses _____.

4. Amber wants _____.

Whose Ball Is Whose?

Four balls were found in the neighborhood. Mr. Smith wants to return them. Can you help him find the owners? Use the clues below to help you. Write the answers on the lines below.

Clues
Glenn loves to play a team game with a goalie.
Fred uses a bat to hit his ball.
Jeff uses his ball to shoot hoops.
Steve knocks things down with his ball.

baseball

soccer ball

bowling ball

basketball

1. Glenn owns the _____.

2. Fred owns the _____.

3. Jeff owns the _____.

4. Steve owns the _____.

Who Lives Where?

Four friends live in different houses in the same neighborhood. The mailman needs to bring their mail to them, but he forgot their house numbers. Use the clues below to help him find out who lives in which house. Write the answers on the lines below.

Clues

Shellee lives in the house with the biggest number.

Bonnie's house number starts with two numbers that are the same.

Karen lives in the house below Shelle's.

Diane lives in the house beside Karen and below Bonnie.

1. Shellee lives at house number _____.

2. Bonnie lives at house number _____.

3. Karen lives at house number _____.

4. Diane lives at house number _____.

What Am I?

The animals got loose in the barnyard. Can you help Emily find out who is who and where they live? Use the clues below to help you. Write the answers on the lines below.

Clues

Porkie likes to roll around in the mud.

Hilda loves to run and nibble grass.

Frannie needs to get back and sit on her eggs.

Kyle loves to eat cheese and hide in small, dark places.

pasture   pigpen

1. Porkie is a _____ and he lives in a _____ .

2. Hilda is a _____ and she lives in the _____ .

3. Frannie is a _____ that lives in a _____ .

4. Kyle is a _____ that lives in the _____ .

Team Spirit

The soccer team is out to win a medal. Can you find out the order in which the four team members kicked the ball to score the winning goal? Use the clues below to help you solve the mystery. Write the nicknames of the players in the order they kicked on the lines below.

Clues

The second player to kick trapped the ball and dribbled up the field. She has her hair in a ponytail.

The last player kicked the ball into the net. She has a star on her shirt.

The goalie kicked the ball first. She is holding the ball.

The player that kicked third is wearing a crown on her head.

| Small Fry | Princess | Jenna Girl | Soccer Girl |

1. Who kicked first? _____

2. Who kicked second? _____

3. Who kicked third? _____

4. Who kicked last? _____

Juggle Away

Each of the jugglers uses different things to practice juggling with. Who likes to juggle with what? Use the clues below to help you. Write the answers on the lines below.

Clues
Ricardo juggles with two things at one time. One is dangerous.
John uses objects that can be knocked down.
Brian likes to juggle with objects that are yellow.
Juan prefers to juggle with things that are round.

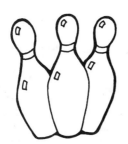

bowling pins

bananas

a sword and ball

apples

1. Ricardo juggles _____.

2. John juggles _____.

3. Brian juggles _____.

4. Juan juggles _____.

Holidays

Four children in Mrs. Russell's class were talking about their favorite holidays. Read the words in the Word Box. Then read the clues below. Write the holiday from the Word Box that each child likes best on the lines below.

Word Box

| birthdays | Easter |
| Fourth of July | Christmas |

Andria loves angels, lights, and trees.

Levi thinks fireworks, picnics, and soccer games are the best.

Oh Joon likes balloons, cake, and presents.

Brandon prefers to hunt for eggs and eat chocolates.

1. Andria loves _____.

2. Levi thinks _____ is the best.

3. Oh Joon likes _____.

4. Brandon prefers _____.

Big Diggers

Four children in Mrs. Ritcher's class were talking about moving dirt around. Read the words from the Word Box. Then, read the clues below. Write the tool from the Word Box that each child chose on the lines below.

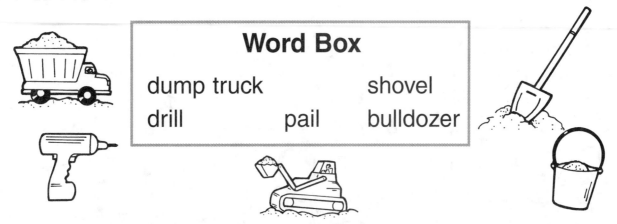

Word Box

dump truck		shovel
drill	pail	bulldozer

Payton said she would need something that made deep, fast holes.

Christopher was sure he would be powerful enough to use something made of wood and metal.

Katie wanted to move small amounts of sand or dirt in a container.

Nick thought driving would be best.

Christina wanted a big machine to push the dirt around.

1. Payton loves the _____.

2. Christopher uses a _____.

3. Katie wants a_____.

4. Nick can't wait to drive a _____.

5. Christina wanted a _____.

Same? Same?

There are many things that are the same in each picture.
Look at each picture carefully and find the items that are the
same. Circle or color them. Can you find them all?

Delightfully Different

There are many things that are different in each picture. Look at each picture carefully and find the items that are different. Circle or color them. Can you find them all?

Picnic Panic

Help! The ants are about to take over the picnic! Look at each picture carefully and find the matching pairs of food items. Circle or color them. Can you save the picnic by finding them all?

Cracker Barrel

Savannah and Seth want to be detectives. Look at the picture long and hard and then cover it. Next, try to answer the questions on the lines below without looking back at the picture. Can you help them remember?

1. How many crackers are in the picture?

   _____

2. What are the shapes of the crackers?

   _____

3. What are the designs on the crackers?

   _____

Ants on Parade

Take a long look at the picture. Try to remember everything you see. Then, cover the picture and try to answer as many questions as you can without looking back at the picture.

1. How many ants are in the parade?

_____

2. What does the ant in shorts have on his head?

_____

3. How many ants are holding the watermelon?

_____

4. Who is leading the parade?

_____

5. What did the short ant drop?

_____

Dump Trucks Everywhere

Look at the picture long and hard. Try to remember everything you see. Then, cover the picture and answer as many questions as you can without looking back at the picture.

1. What is in the large dump truck?

   _____

2. How many dump trucks are full of corn?

   _____

3. What is the striped dump truck dumping out?

   _____

4. How many dump trucks are there in all?

   _____

5. What is the driver of the large dump truck wearing?

   _____

Concentration Cereal

Take a long look at the picture. Try to remember everything you see. Then, cover the picture and answer the questions on the lines below. No peeking!

1. How many of the bowls have spoons?

_____

2. How many children are in the picture?

_____

3. How many bowls have bananas in them?

_____

4. What is the word in one of the bowls?

_____

5. How many cups are in the picture?

_____

6. How many cereal bowls are there?

_____

Playground Caper

Jasmine is having a hard time finding the hidden pictures. There is a list of pictures to find at the bottom of the page. Circle or color each object in the picture that you find from the list. Can you help her find all ten?

sandwich	grapes	pear	bread	hamburger
chicken leg	soda can	carrot	apple	banana

Zoom, Zoom, Beep, Beep

Alex is having a hard time finding the hidden pictures. There is a list of pictures to find at the bottom of the page. Circle or color each object in the picture that you find from the list. Can you help him find all ten?

hammer	saw	bucket	nails	hard hat
tractor	drill	tool box	boot	glue bottle

70

Food Galore

Tanya is having a hard time finding the hidden pictures. There is a list of pictures to find at the bottom of the page. Circle or color each object from the list that you find. Can you help her find all ten?

| pencil | jump rope | markers | paper | book |
| chair | desk | lunch tray | rubber ball | pen |

Out-of-Sight Farming

Travis is having a hard time finding the hidden pictures. There is a list of pictures to find at the bottom of the page. Circle or color each object from the list that you find. Can you help him find all ten?

pig	chicken	duck	horse	pitchfork
cow	rabbit	barn	farmer	tractor

Land, Water, Air

Kelly is having a hard time finding the hidden pictures. Listed in the box below is a list of all the hidden pictures she needs to find. Circle or color each object from the list that you find. Can you help her find all ten?

train	wagon	van	boat	tricycle
plane	hot air balloon	car	bike	bus

Can You See It?

Joshua and Kyle are having a hard time finding the hidden pictures. There is a list of pictures to find at the bottom of the page. Circle or color each object from the list that you find. Can you help them find all ten?

toothbrush	hair brush	comb	teddy bear	slippers
toothpaste	pajamas	shirt	sleeping bag	pants

Got Ya!

Ymari is having a hard time finding the hidden pictures. There is a list of pictures to find at the bottom of the page. Circle or color each object from the list that you find. Can you help her find all ten?

shoe	shirt	rain jacket	mittens	boots
sock	pants	umbrella	sweater	hat

Pirates on the Sail

Write a strange story to share with your friends. Fill in the blanks below, but do not look ahead at the story. Then, use the words to complete your strange tale. Read the story to someone you love!

1. month of year _____	6. food _____
2. an illness _____	7. action word _____
3. name of a place _____	8. action word _____
4. name of a person _____	9. name of a thing _____
5. food _____	10. food _____

   One cloudy, stormy day in _____ , Frankie

woke up with a _____ . His mother made him stay
                             2

in _____ all day. He fell asleep dreaming about
   3

pirates. Suddenly, a loud pirate named _____
                                          4

shook him and told him to eat sloppy _____
                                          5

and hard _____ for breakfast. Another angry
                      6

pirate made him _____ over large pillows and
                                7

_____ beanbags across his bedroom. A
               8

third pirate grabbed him out of bed and made him get on the

great big _____ and sail the high seas. The
                      9

waves were crashing. All of a sudden, Frankie's mom shook

him awake. She scared off the mean pirates and fed him

_____ for lunch! He was safe from danger now!
   10

Cat Fight

Write a strange story to share with your friends. Fill in the blanks below, but do not look ahead at the story. Then, use the words to complete your strange tale.

1. kitchen tool _____

2. loud noise _____

3. day of the week _____

4. boy's name _____

5. boy's name _____

6. shape (more than one) _____

7. one body part of a cat _____

8. a last name _____

9. food (more than one) _____

10. animal sound _____

11. food (from #9) _____

Grab the _____ ! Crash! Bang! Boom!

_____ ! On _____
          2   3

afternoon, noises were coming from everywhere! Two large

cats were fighting on the street corner. The biggest cat,

_____ , was mad at the smaller cat,
          4

_____ . Both cats wanted to play in the
          5

empty lot at the corner. They spit at each other. They ran in

_____ . A _____ was flying
          6   7

in all directions! Suddenly, up came the big cat's owner,

Mr. _____ . Both cats saw the two
          8

_____ in his hands. He grinned at them.
          9

Enough fighting, boys! They _____ sweetly.
                                              10

The _____ looked better than the fight!
          11

Princess Diary

Write a strange story to share with your friends. Fill in the blanks below, but do not look ahead at the story. Then, use the words to complete your strange tale.

1. girl's name _____

2. candy _____

3. part of a house _____

4. part of a book _____

5. action word (ending in -ing)

_____

6. action word (ending in -ed)

_____

7. name_____

8. girl's name (from #1)_____

   "Someone has read and destroyed my diary!" wailed

Princess _____ . "They will know all of my

secrets!" She was the princess of _____
                        1

Land. Her diary lay by the open _____ .
                        2

Pages were ripped out and torn. Who could have done such
                        3

an awful thing? Even the _____ was torn

out. She went _____ through the castle!
                        4

She called the magicians and all of her father's servants. No
                        5

one knew who _____ her diary. They all
                        6

stopped their jobs and went to help the princess. "Come

here!" shouted the butler. Her dog _____ was
                        7

under the bushes in the garden. The pages were still between

his teeth. He looked guilty! The mystery was solved and

Princess _____ had to start a new diary!
                        8

She sighed; at least her secrets were safe with the dog!

Sir Knight in Shining Armor

Write a strange story to share with your friends. Fill in the blanks below, but do not look ahead at the story. Then, use the words to complete your strange tale.

1. object in the sky _____   _____
2. day of the week _____
7. three kind words _____
3. material used to build things
8. action word _____
   _____
9. describing word _____
4. bright color _____
10. something that gives light (more than one) _____
5. color _____
6. animal sound (ending in -ing)
11. place _____

A _____ shone over the castle one summery

_____ night. Sir Knight rode up to the
2

_____ castle on his new _____horse.
3   4

His armor was shiny and made of strong metal. A window

was open in the far tower. A maiden with _____
5

hair was looking out the window, waiting for the knight to come.

The horse made a loud _____ sound. Sir Knight
6

rode below the maiden's window and softly whispered,

"_____" to her. The princess _____
7   8

down a silk rope and climbed onto the back of his

_____ horse. All the _____
9   10

in the castle went on, but the princess rode off into the night

with Sir Knight in Shining Armor to _____.
11

Terrible, Awful, Very Bad Day!

Write a strange story to share with your friends. Fill in the blanks below, but do not look ahead at the story. Then, use the words to complete your strange tale.

1. object in a bedroom _____
2. girl's name _____
3. body part _____
4. day of the week _____
5. insect or bug (more than one)

_____

6. messy food _____
7. piece of clothing _____
8. piece of clothing _____
9. house pet _____
10. vehicle_____
11. action word _____

Thump! The _____ hit _____

                             1   2

on the _____ when she first got out of bed on

                3

_____ morning! Her brother put _____

        4   5

in her cereal bowl, and she spilled _____

                                                              6

on her new _____ . Her _____

                     7   8

wouldn't fit right. Then, her _____ ate her

                                             9

sandwich before she left for school. The _____

                                                                         10

was late to pick her up. This was going to be an awful day!

She could just feel it; so she decided to _____ .

                                                                             11

Elephant King

Write a strange story to share with your friends. Fill in the blanks below, but do not look ahead at the story. Then, use the words to complete your strange tale.

1. color _____	8. kind of vegetables_____
2. boy's name _____	9. kind of vegetables_____
3. body part _____	10. kind of candy _____
4. place _____	11. kind of candy _____
5. funny action word _____	12. body part _____
6. action word (ending in -ing)	13. building _____
_____	14. fruit _____
7. kind of fruit _____	

A large, _____ coconut fell off the tree and
                         1

hit _____ , the Elephant King, right on the
             2

_____ . He was on his way to the _____
    3   4

to _____ . His servants saw him _____
      5   6

and ran to see if he was feeling all right. The king started to

talk really funny. " _____ and _____ ".
                      7   8

" _____ and _____ ." "King,
       9   10

whatever is the matter?" they all asked at once. He screamed,

"Jumping _____ my _____ hurts all
            11   12

over!" They rushed him to the animal _____ ,
                                         13

and the nurse gave him a shot of _____
                                     14

juice. He jumped off the table and never hurt again!

Imaginary Kingdom

Write a strange story to share with your friends. Fill in the blanks below, but do not look ahead at the story. Then, use the words to complete your strange tale.

1. animal _____

2. candy _____

3. shape _____

4. candy _____

5. type of coin (more than one)

   _____

6. vehicle (more than one)

   _____

7. kind of food_____

8. kind of food_____

9. vegetable (more than one)

   _____

10. day of the week _____

11. game _____

12. song _____

Twinky, the _____ , lived in a _____
1   2
kingdom under Katrina's bed. The kingdoom had lovely, tall

_____ buildings and houses made out of
3

_____ . The streets were made of
4

_____ all in neat rows. All the animals used
5

_____ to get around. The city was full of
6

beautiful _____ and _____ .
7   8
No one ever got tired of eating _____ . Each
9

_____ everyone met to play _____
10   11

and sing _____ . It was a wonderful place
12

to visit or live!

Veggie Tales

Look at the groups of words below the Word Box. Each of them is a clue describing a different vegetable. Read each clue and decide which vegetable it is describing. Write the vegetables from the Word Box on the lines below.

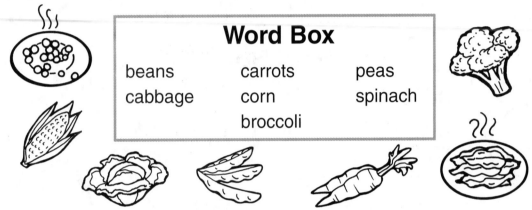

Word Box

beans	carrots	peas
cabbage	corn	spinach
	broccoli	

1. Looks like seaweed, is green and slimy

_____

2. Is green, looks like a little tree, has a stem

_____

3. Is round, squishy, and small

_____

4. Can be large or small, are orange, and have a green top

_____

5. Is large and round, is rubbery, and can be green or purple

_____

6. Are long and thin, and usually green

_____

7. Is not round, usually sweet, and mostly yellow

_____

Table Talk

Look at the groups of words below the Word Box. Each of them is a clue describing a different item to use on your dinner table. Read each clue and decide which table item it is describing. Write the items from the Word Box on the lines below.

Word Box		
spoon	fork	plate
cup	napkin	knife

1. Has three or four sharp points on one end

_____

2. Is used to wipe your mouth, and has a rectangle shape

_____

3. Is long, thin, and has sharp bumps on one side at the end

_____

4. Is round and flat, like a circle

_____

5. Is long, with a circle on the end, used for cereal or yogurt

_____

6. Is tall and holds things to drink

_____

Sports Stuff

Look at the groups of words below the Word Box. Each of them is a clue describing a different sport. Read each clue and decide which sport it is describing. Write the sports from the Word Box on the lines below.

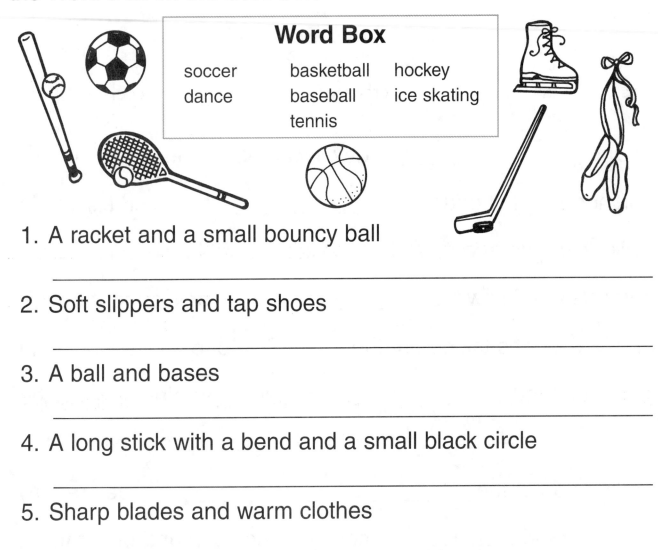

Word Box

soccer	basketball	hockey
dance	baseball	ice skating
	tennis	

1. A racket and a small bouncy ball

_____

2. Soft slippers and tap shoes

_____

3. A ball and bases

_____

4. A long stick with a bend and a small black circle

_____

5. Sharp blades and warm clothes

_____

6. Large orange ball and a net

_____

7. Black and white ball and a net

_____

In My Neighborhood

Look at the words in the Word Box below. Then, read the story below and write the correct words from the Word Box in the blanks. Cross out each word as you use it. Then, read the story to a friend.

Word Box			
door	cars	mail carrier	sunny
gas station		grocery store	school

One _____ day, I wanted to take a walk in my
_____1_____

neighborhood. I opened the _____ and started to
_____2_____

walk down the street. At first, it was very quiet because it was

early. Soon, I saw the _____ delivering the mail,
_____3_____

and Mrs. Jones taking out the trash. The birds were singing in

the trees, and _____ were turning to go to the
_____4_____

freeway. At the corner, I saw that there were many people

getting gas at the _____ before they
_____5_____

drove to work. Ladies and men were going in and out of the

_____ with sacks of food. Suddenly, I
_____6_____

looked at my watch. 8:00! I needed to get home and get my

backpack. It was time for _____!
_____7_____

That's My Job

Look at the words in the Word Box below. Then, read the story about Robert below and write the correct words from the Word Box in the blanks. Cross out each word as you use it. Then, read the story to a friend.

Word Box

baker	police officer	sweeper
dentist	trash collector	secretary

"What will I be when I grow up?" I thought in my dream. My car was driving fast on a long, dark street looking for the bad guys. I must be a _____ . Suddenly, my dream changed to a big, noisy truck with lots of green bags and trash cans. Maybe I was a _____ . Lights started to flash, and I was in a little white truck with a small shiny, flashing light. Faster and faster I drove, making circles in a parking lot and sweeping up people's messes at shopping centers. I was a _____ . As quick as a flash, I was typing papers and working on a computer. I answered the phone. Was I a _____ ? Time for a coffee break. The smell was sweet. Chocolate frosting and chocolate cake was on the table. Was I a _____ ? Then, there was a tap on my arm…"Wake up Robert!" I sat up in the chair. My mouth was open. I looked into the eyes of my _____ ! I had fallen asleep in the chair!

In My Room

Look at the words in the Word Box below. Read the story below and write the correct words from the Word Box in the blanks. Cross out each word as you use it. Then, read the story to a friend.

Word Box			
tennis shoes	bed	lamp	chair
bookshelf	stuffed animal	smelly socks	

I love my bedroom! There is a _____ 1 in

the corner for all my favorite books. My comfortable

_____ 2 sits in the corner, and I love to sit in it

with a good book. The spotted animal_____ 3

gives me light to read, and my _____ 4 is where

I sleep each night, snuggling deep under my warm blankets. I

throw my _____ 5 and _____ 6

under my bed and hope that my mom doesn't see them. Last,

I always keep my _____ 7 next to my pillow at

night to keep me safe! My room is my favorite place to be

when I want to be quiet and alone.

"Ate" in All

Read the clues below. Each of the words being described ends with "ate." Choose the word from the Word Box that is being described and write it on the line. Good luck!

Word Box		
gate	plate	skate
date	hate	late

1. Not on time: _____

2. On a fence: _____

3. Used to eat on: _____

4. Done on ice: _____

5. Do not like: _____

6. A day on the calendar: _____

"Ake" in All

Read the clues below. Each of the words being described ends with "ake." Choose the word from the Word Box that is being described and write it on the line. Good luck!

Word Box

cake	rake	bake
fake	quake	lake

1. Can do in an oven:_____

2. For birthdays: _____

3. A place to swim:_____

4. For picking up leaves: _____

5. Shakes the earth:_____

6. Not real: _____

90

Answer Key

Who's Driving 20? (p. 4)

Car 1=17

Car 2=18

Car 3=20 (should be colored)

Car 4=17

Car 5=25

Car 6=13

Crazy Canisters (p. 5)

99, 93, 85, 77, 38, 21, 20

Shapes All Over (p. 6)

Triangles: 10

Hexagons: 5

Squares: 4

Farm Squabble (p. 7)

	1	2	3	4	5	6
pigs	▓	▓	▓			
cows	▓	▓	▓	▓		
sheep	▓	▓	▓		▓	▓
chickens	▓	▓	▓	▓	▓	
dogs	▓	▓				

1. sheep
2. 4
3. 20

Pirate Pete's Buried Treasure (p. 8)

Stompin' Boots (p. 9)

1. $7 + \boxed{5} = 12$
2. $11 - \boxed{6} = 5$
3. $5 + \boxed{4} = 9$
4. $15 - \boxed{10} = 5$
5. $9 + \boxed{2} = 11$
6. $10 - \boxed{8} = 2$

Math Wizard (p. 10)

Start ⇒ $5 - 2 = 3 + 1 = 4$

$4 + 3 = 3 - 6 = 2 + =$

$7 - 1 = 6 - 2 = 4 + 1$

$10 = 1 + 9 = 4 + 5 = -$

$2 = 8 - 3 = 5$ Finish!

Can You Dew It? (p. 11)

7 children	$7 + 4 = 11$
6 puddles	$10 - 6 = 4$
10 raindrops	$5 + 4 = 9$
4 rain boots	$6 - 4 = 2$
5 umbrellas	
4 raincoats	

Bubba's Books (p. 12)

1. If You Give a Moose a Muffin
2. Junnie B. Jones Smells Something Fishy
3. Stage Fright
4. Trouble with Friends
5. When Momma Comes Home Tonight

Beach Days (p. 13)

1. Getting out of bed in the morning
2. Packing swimsuit
3. Driving to the beach
4. Playing on beach—picnic lunch
5. Showering off sand
6. Watching the sunset

Who's First to the Movies? (p. 14)

Sam, Sandy, Sally, and Sarah

Watch Out for the Watches! (p. 15)

12:00, 1:30, 2:00, 5:30, 6:00, 7:00

Confusing Candies (p. 16)

20¢, 38¢, 39¢, 45¢, 55¢, 72¢

Numbers Gone Wild! (p. 17)

29, 33, 42, 44, 56, 77, 100

Month Mania (p. 18)

January, February, March, April, May, June, July, August, September, October, November, December

Answer Key *(cont.)*

Pizza Puzzler (p. 19)

Piece C is the missing piece. It should be circled.

Matching Cans (p. 20)

Black heart-white heart

Black star-white star

Black circle-white circle

Black oval-white oval

Black diamond-white diamond

Black triangle-white triangle

Black hexagon-white hexagon

What Comes Next? (p. 21)

1. 123123
2. circle
3. corn
4. spoon
5. peas

Maybelle's Quilt (p. 22)

Billy's Hideout (p. 23)

1.

2.

3.

4.

5.

Cookies Like This! (p. 24)

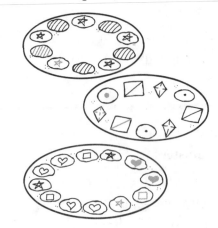

Skip It! (p. 25)

1. 5, <u>10</u>, 15, <u>20</u>, 25, <u>30</u>, <u>35</u>, 40, <u>45</u>, 50
2. 10, 20, 30, 40, <u>50</u>, <u>60</u>, 70, <u>80</u>, <u>90</u>, 100
3. 24, <u>26</u>, 28, 30, <u>32</u>, <u>34</u>, 36, <u>38</u>, <u>40</u>, <u>42</u>, 44, 46, <u>48</u>, 50
4. 25, <u>30</u>, 35, <u>40</u>, <u>45</u>, 50, <u>55</u>, <u>60</u>, <u>65</u>, 70

It's Your Ball (p. 26)

1. A
2. A
3. B

Cloud Bursters (p. 27)

1. B   3. A
2. A   4. B

Cracking Up Over Patterns (p. 28)

1. plate
2. pail
3. ballet shoes
4. napkin
5. lightning bolt

Mama Tree (p. 29)

Stop needling each other!

Snowman's Good Grades (p. 30)

He was a snow – it – all!

Hummingbirds (p. 31)

Because they've forgotten the words.

Frog Drink (p. 32)

Hot croako

Answer Key *(cont.)*

Frog Wear (p. 33)

Open-toad sandals

Fishing for Toast (p. 34)

A jelly fish.

Snowflake Students (p. 35)

They keep drifting off.

Sparrow in the Library (p. 36)

He was looking for the bookworm.

Words in Words (p. 37)

Some possible answers are:
ten, cent, tear, pen, trap, tree, pea, car, tar, part, rent, net, pet, rant, carp, ant, carpet, ran, pan, tan, trap, partner, pant, peer, cart, can, tap, parent, care, pear, ape, tape, cape

Scrambled Up Zoo (p. 38)

monkey, lion, tiger, hippo, giraffe, gorilla, dolphin

What's the Same? (p. 39)

Column 1 – th letters; four-letter words

Column 2 – ou letters

Column 3 – all the same letters in different orders; four-letter words

Column 4 – the letter i

Column 5 – all words rhyme; long e sound

Baking Poem (p. 40)

mud, thing, sing, hip, day, please, chips, mix, tin, pack, mud, down, pies, week, cake

Animal Language (p. 41)

1. C   3. B   5. B
2. A   5. A

In the Barn (p. 42)

hay, chicken, barn, tractor, fence, horse, farmer, cow, pigs, milk

Tell the Truth (p. 43)

Sentence number 2 is the correct sentence. It should be circled.

Corrections to make each sentence true.

1. four   5. green   8. 26
2. (true sentence) 6. down   9. vowels
3. blue   7. brown   10. two
4. rectangle

Alphabet Soup (p. 44

The word "FROM" is not in the bowl of soup.

Earthworms (p. 45)

Some possible answers are:
earth, worms, heart, hearts, smart, storm, more, sore, tore, wore, war, tar, what, hat, sat, rat, mat, eat, eats, art, mart, swat, tear, roar, wart, was, saw, horse, heat, seat, meat, the, star, them, row, home, wear, team, ram, ham

Tangled Ropes (p. 46)

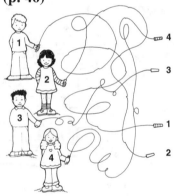

I Scream! You Scream! We All Scream for Ice Cream! (p. 47)

House on Fire! (p. 48)

Answer Key *(cont.)*

To the Top of the Mast! (p. 49)

RRR!!! Race'em! (p. 50)

Car 1 – 3rd Place

Car 2 – 2nd Place

Car 3 – 1st Place

Star Search (p. 51)

Line 3

Beaver Dam (p. 52)

Who's Up First? (p. 53)

1. Filbert
2. Frankie
3. Freddy
4. Fernando

What's Your Flavor? (p. 54)

1. You get <u>Strawberry Crunch</u>.
2. Jennifer likes <u>Chocolate Chunk</u>.
3. Ashley chooses an <u>Ice Cream Sandwich</u>.
4. Amber wants <u>Vanilla Caramel</u>.

Whose Ball Is Whose? (p. 55)

1. Glenn owns the <u>soccer ball</u>.
2. Fred owns the <u>baseball</u>.
3. Jeff owns the <u>basketball</u>.
4. Steve owns the <u>bowling ball</u>.

Who Lives Where? (p. 56)

1. Shellee lives at <u>9321</u>.
2. Bonnie lives at <u>2276</u>.
3. Karen lives at <u>3793</u>.
4. Diane lives at <u>1269</u>.

What Am I? (p. 57)

1. Porkie is a <u>pig</u> and he lives in a <u>pigpen</u>.
2. Hilda is a <u>horse</u> and she lives in the <u>pasture</u>.
3. Frannie is a <u>chicken</u> who lives in a <u>chicken coop</u>.
4. Klye is a <u>mouse</u> that lives in the <u>mouse hole</u>.

Team Spirit (p. 58)

1. Soccer Girl
2. Small Fry
3. Princess
4. Jenna Girl

Juggle Away (p. 59)

1. Ricardo juggles <u>a sword and ball</u>.
2. John juggles <u>bowling pins</u>.
3. Brian juggles <u>bananas</u>.
4. Juan juggles <u>apples</u>.

Holidays (p. 60)

1. Andria loves <u>Christmas</u>.
2. Levi thinks <u>Fourth of July</u> is the best.
3. Oh Joon likes <u>birthdays</u>.
4. Brandon prefers <u>Easter</u>.

Big Diggers (p. 61)

1. Payton loves the <u>drill</u>.
2. Christopher uses a <u>shovel</u>.
3. Katie wants a <u>pail</u>.
4. Nick can't wait to drive a <u>dump truck</u>.
5. Christina wanted a <u>bulldozer</u>.

Same? Same? (p. 62)

Things that are the same:

smiley face on food stand

girl in front of food stand

large heart balloon

ball on sand

boy with surfboard

Answer Key (cont.)

Same? Same? (p. 62) *cont.*

birds in sky

boat in water

girl on bench holding drink

bucket on sand

Delightfully Different (p. 63)

Things that are different:

girl's shirt with happy face, girl's shirt without happy face

one picture has a sun rising—other has a sun setting

one has three suitcases—other has two

suitcase with flowers, suitcase without flowers

one picture has plane flying—other does not

Picnic Panic (p. 64)

Matching food items:

pretzel, apple, chicken leg on napkin, watermelon, bag of chips

Cracker Barrel (p. 65)

1. 15
2. heart, star, rectangle
3. hearts have many dots, stars have nothing, rectangles have one large dot

Ants on Parade (p. 66)

1. 10
2. a cake
3. three
4. the queen ant
5. a large bowl that has something in it

Dump Trucks Everywhere (p. 67)

1. carrots
2. two
3. bananas
4. six
5. sunglasses

Concentration Cereal (p. 68)

1. five
2. two
3. two
4. APPLE
5. four
6. nine

Playground Caper (p. 69)

Zoom, Zoom, Beep, Beep (p. 70)

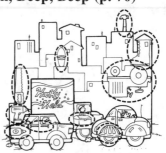

Food Galore (p. 71)

Out-of-Sight Farming (p. 72)

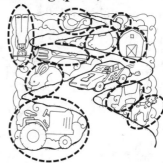

Land, Water, Air (p. 73)

Answer Key (cont.)

Can You See It? (p. 74)

Got Ya! (p. 75)

Strange but Amazing Stories (pages 76–82)

Answers are different for each child. Encourage them to use word banks, dictionaries, or any other source available to help them.

Veggie Tales (p. 83)

1. spinach
2. broccoli
3. peas
4. carrots
5. cabbage
6. beans
7. corn

Table Talk (p. 84)

1. fork
2. napkin
3. knife
4. plate
5. spoon
6. cup

Sports Stuff (p. 85)

1. tennis
2. dance
3. baseball
4. hockey
5. ice skating
6. basketball
7. soccer

In My Neighborhood (p. 86)

1. sunny
2. door
3. mail carrier
4. cars
5. gas station
6. grocery store
7. school

That's My Job (p. 87)

1. police officer
2. trash collector
3. sweeper
4. secretary
5. baker
6. dentist

In My Room (p. 88)

1. bookshelf
2. chair
3. lamp
4. bed
5. and 6. tennis shoes, smelly socks
7. stuffed animal

"Ate" in All (p. 89)

1. late
2. gate
3. plate
4. skate
5. hate
6. date

"Ake" in All (p. 90)

1. bake
2. cake
3. lake
4. rake
5. quake
6. fake